D0600647

Moorcroft, Christine.
The Taj Mahal /
c1998.
33305013148964
MH 02/08/00
WITHDRAWN

GREAT BUILDINGS

THE TAJ MAHAL

Christine Moorcroft

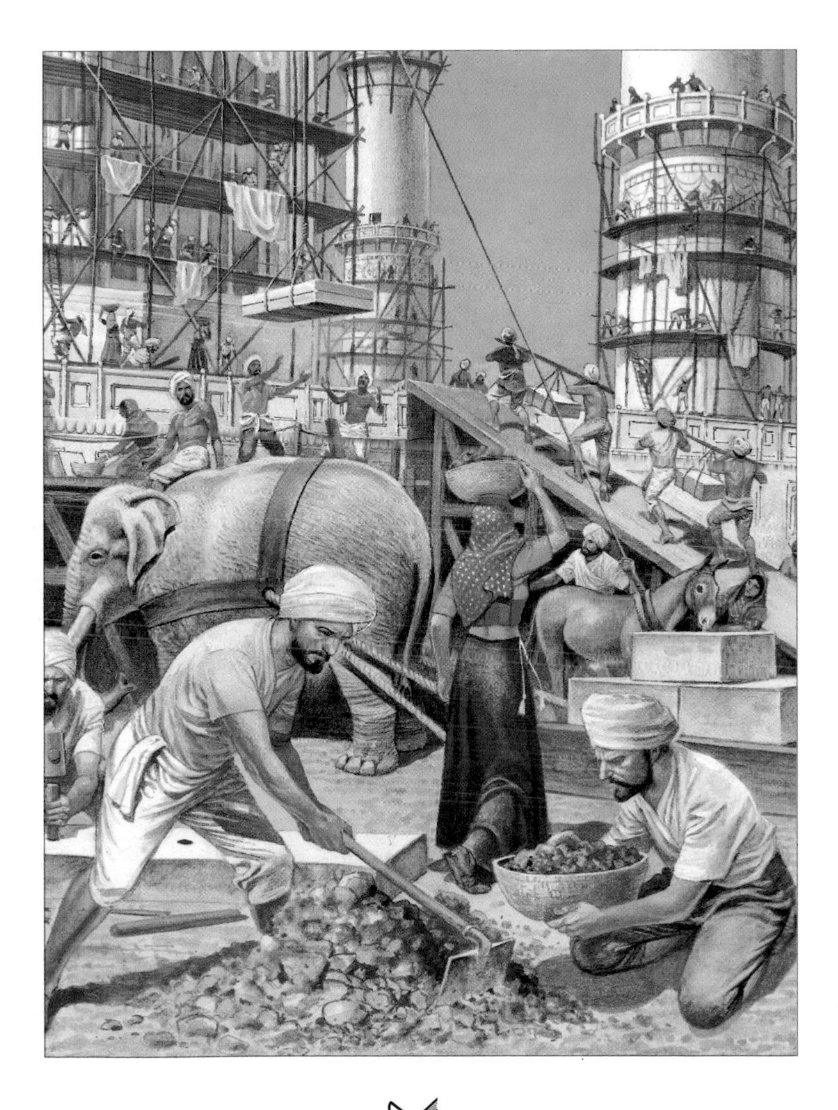

RSVP
RAINTREE STECK-VAUGHN PUBLISHERS
The Steck-Vaughn Company

SANTA CLARA COUNTY LIBRARY
3 3305 01314 8964

GREAT BUILDINGS

THE COLOSSEUM

THE EMPIRE STATE BUILDING

THE GREAT PYRAMID

THE HOUSES OF PARLIAMENT

THE PARTHENON

THE TAJ MAHAL

© Copyright 1998, text, Steck-Vaughn Company

All rights reserved. No part of this book may be reproduced or utilized in any form or by any means, electronic or mechanical, including photocopying, recording, or by any information storage and retrieval system, without permission in writing from the Publisher. Inquiries should be addressed to: Copyright Permissions, Steck-Vaughn Company, P.O. Box 26015, Austin, TX 78755.

Published by Raintree Steck-Vaughn Publishers,
an imprint of Steck-Vaughn Company

Library of Congress Cataloging-in-Publication Data
Moorcraft, Christine.
The Taj Mahal/ Christine Moorcraft.
p. cm.—(Great buildings)
Includes bibliographical references and index.
Summary: Examines the design and construction of the architectural masterpiece that was built during the Mogul rule of India.
ISBN 0-8172-4920-6
1. Taj Mahal (Agra, India)—Juvenile literature.
2. Architecture, Mogul—India—Agra—Juvenile literature.
3. Agra (India)—Buildings, structures, etc.—Juvenile literature.
[1. Taj Mahal (Agra, India).]
I. Title. II. Series.
NA6008.A33M66 1998
726'.8'09542—dc21 96-15619

Printed in Italy. Bound in the United States.
1 2 3 4 5 6 7 8 9 0 02 01 00 99 98

Illustrations: Mike White
Maps: Peter Bull

CONTENTS

A FUNERAL

Late in December 1631, a solemn funeral procession arrived in the city of Agra. There were elephants decorated with gold and velvet cloths and cavalrymen with flags, riding their fine horses. Leading the procession was the fifteen-year-old Prince Shah Shuja with Wazir Khan, the Royal Physician, and Sati-un-nissa, the Head Stewardess of the Royal Household. They rode in howdahs on the backs of elephants and wore the white clothes of mourning. In the funeral bier at the center of the procession was the body of Empress Mumtaz Mahal, mother of Prince Shuja and beloved wife of Shah Jahan, ruler of the Mogul empire.

Six months earlier, Mumtaz Mahal had died in childbirth at Bhurhanpur, about 435 mi. (700 km) south of Agra. Despite being in advanced pregnancy, she had accompanied Shah Jahan on a military campaign, as was her custom. Stricken with grief at her death, the emperor ordered his entire kingdom into mourning. According to Muslim practice, Mumtaz Mahal's body was buried immediately in Bhurhanpur. Six months later, it was brought to the capital, Agra, to rest in a temporary crypt in a leafy grove on the banks of the Yamuna River.

▲ This red sandstone building in the gardens of the Taj Mahal is where Mumtaz Mahal's body was laid to rest while the great mausoleum was being built.

Emperor Shah Jahan had chosen the most lovely site for his wife's final resting place. But his plans to commemorate her were grander still. Mumtaz Mahal's tomb was to be encased in a building of breathtaking beauty, an eternal monument to an eternal love: the Taj Mahal.

CHAPTER ONE

THE MOGULS IN INDIA

The Moguls were Muslim warriors who came to India from central Asia. In 1519, Babur, a prince from the land now known as Tajikistan, fought his way through the pass between the Hindu Kush Mountains and the Himalayas. In 1526, with an army of just 12,000 men, he defeated the North Indian ruler Sultan Ibrahim, whose own army numbered 100,000, and captured Hindustan and the cities of Agra and Delhi.

Babur, a descendant of the Mongol warlords Genghis Khan and Tamerlane, was the first great Mogul emperor. He disliked India, describing it as "charmless and disorderly." Perhaps in an attempt to impose order he created formal gardens planted with trees and flowers. Babur drew comfort from these cool, green places with their pools, waterfalls, and fountains.

◀ The order and symmetry of Mogul gardens are shown in this contemporary illustration. Here Babur (in the yellow coat) plans a garden near Jalalabad.

Babur's son Humayun succeeded him in 1530. He had no interest in military matters, and he lost large areas of the empire as a result (although he managed to regain these by the time he died). By 1540, Sher Khan, the Afghan ruler of Bihar, had taken control of Hindustan and driven Humayun into exile in Sind. Here Humayun's first son, Akbar, was born.

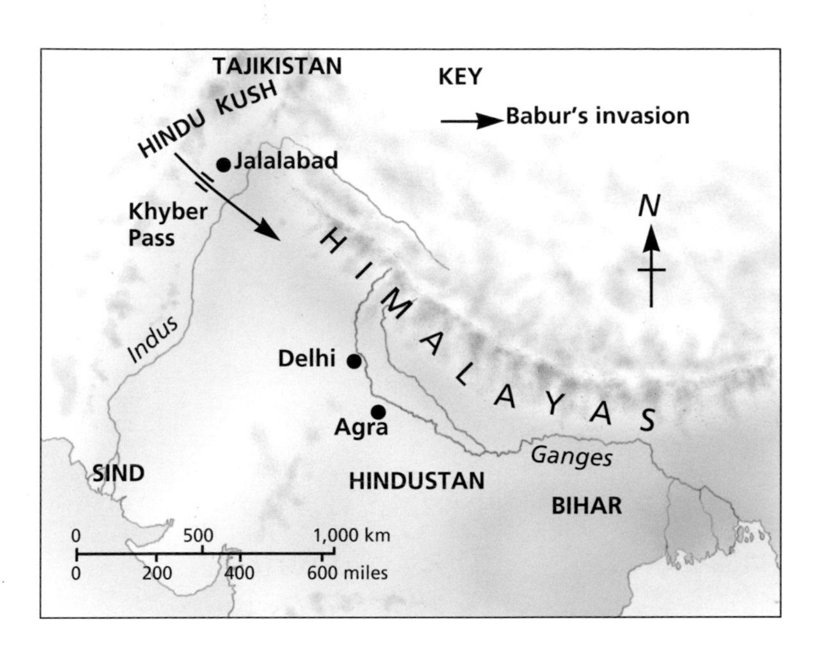

▲ This map shows the route along which Babur marched into India. It also shows Hindustan, the region he conquered.

Akbar was the next great Mogul emperor. An energetic and brilliant soldier, he generally tried to extend the empire by making alliances rather than by shedding blood. Unlike his predecessors, Akbar treated people of different races and religions equally. This way, he succeeded in governing even the proud Hindu rajas who ruled the desert lands of Rajputana. His Muslim ancestors had made Hindus pay a poll tax, but Akbar abolished this; instead, he worked out a fair land tax, which everyone paid, based on what they could earn from their land.

In 1605, Akbar died and was succeeded by his son, Salim, who took the name Jahangir, meaning "the World Seizer." Jahangir was the father of Shah Jahan.

The Akbarnama

Abu-l Fazl, a historian and member of Akbar's court, wrote a biography of the emperor's life called the *Akbarnama*. This illustrated chronicle described palace life and included references to Akbar's many victories. This picture of the siege of Ranthambor shows the ruthless way in which the Moguls dealt with their opponents.

▼ The Red Fort at Agra was built of sandstone. The walls are nearly 70 ft. (21 m) high in places and stretch in a semicircle for 1.5 mi. (2.4 km).

The Moguls' passion for architecture was one of their most enduring legacies to India. Akbar, Jahangir, and Shah Jahan drew upon the artistic richness of their Persian heritage and combined it with the skills of Indian craftspeople. With this unique combination, they succeeded in forging a completely new architectural style.

> "(The stones) were so joined together that the end of a hair could not find a place between them."
>
> Abu-l Fazl, describing the walls of the Red Fort at Agra.

Manufacturing under the Moguls
Akbar encouraged India's manufacturing industry, especially textiles. When fashions from abroad became sought after by the rich, Akbar encouraged carpet weavers from Persia (Iran) and Turan (Turkestan) to settle in India and set up workshops in the royal cities of Agra, Lahore, and Fatehpur Sikri. In the same way, over a thousand Kashmiri shawl workshops opened in Lahore.

▼ About 23 mi. (37 km) northwest of Agra, Akbar founded a new city, Fatehpur Sikri, with its Great Mosque and palaces. The city was built in tribute to a sage who predicted that Akbar would eventually father a son and heir. Fatehpur Sikri took only four years (from 1570 to 1574) to build, but in 1585 it was abandoned and never again occupied.

Akbar oversaw immense building projects: huge forts at Agra, Lahore, and Allahabad, and the capital city of Fatehpur Sikri. As the emperor moved from his fort in one city to another, the entire government of the country moved with him. The forts were small cities for the emperor and his retinue, which included his family, ministers of state, harem, and servants.

> "The cup was of gold, set all over with small turquoises and rubies, the cover the same set with great turquoises, rubies, and emeralds....The value I knew not... but they [the stones] are in number about 2,000 and in gold about 20 ounces [about 560 grams]."
>
> British ambassador Sir Thomas Roe, describing a cup presented to him by Shah Jahan in 1616.

Life in Mogul India ranged between two extremes: vast wealth and grinding poverty. The emperors flaunted their riches and power, perhaps most conspicuously in the solid-gold ceilings and jewel-encrusted walls of their buildings. Huge quantities of luxury goods were used at court. Pictures from the time show members of the imperial family riding elephants adorned with embroidered cloths and jeweled headbands. Their jewelry included pendants, bracelets, and turban ornaments. Even household utensils like spoons and the handles of swords and daggers were studded with jewels.

▶ The courtiers in this illustration are enjoying a musical interlude at a wedding celebration. Most of the men have their gowns wrapped to the right, which indicates that they are Muslim.

◀ This gold spoon set with jewels dates from Akbar's reign.

At court, men always dressed formally, wearing *jama* (long gowns) made of printed and dyed cotton, wrapped to the right if they were Muslim and at the left if they were Hindu; under this would be worn *paijama*, loose-fitting trousers that tapered toward the ankles. Around the waist would be tied a *patka* (sash). They always wore turbans with gold or jeweled ornaments.

A woman of the court would wear a tight-fitting *choli* (bodice), sometimes of transparent material, and *paijama*. Over this she would wear a long transparent *pesvaj* (coat) of thin material. She, too, wore a *patka* and would have an *odhni* (scarf) draped around her shoulders.

However, most of the people in Mogul India lived as they had always done, in thatched houses with mud walls, scratching a living from the land. The taxes they paid could be between a third and half of their income. In the country and in cities the poor lived in one-room dwellings that housed whole families.

▲ Emperor Akbar (at the top of the illustration in a white gown) directs building work at Fatehpur Sikri. Working people usually wore clothes made of pieces of plain white cotton, although here they are also shown wearing knee-length gowns made of plain dyed cloth.

CHAPTER TWO

A GREAT LOVE

"(He will be) more resplendent than the sun."

"The citadels of glory the new-born is destined to conquer."

Astrologers on the birth of Prince Khurram

In 1592, in Agra, a son was born to Prince Salim and one of his wives, Jodh Bai, a Hindu princess. The child was given the name Khurram (meaning "joyous") by his grandfather, Akbar. Although Khurram was not the eldest of his grandsons, Akbar chose him to carry out his hopes for the future.

Akbar employed learned tutors to teach Khurram at the school of the royal mosque, but he was the young prince's real teacher, taking him hunting and showing him how to use weapons. He told him stories about heroic battles he had fought, about the glory of the empire, and how to be a great ruler. When Akbar died, the boy was so distressed that he refused to leave his grandfather's room until the body was taken away for the funeral.

◀ Jahangir inherited from Akbar an empire that took "two years travel with caravan" to cross. His likeness, with a wine cup, is stamped on this gold coin.

After Akbar's death, Khurram became his father's favorite son and most trusted adviser. Prince Salim, who had now become the Emperor Jahangir, had a special throne made for him. In his memoirs Jahangir calls Khurram "in all respects the first of my sons."

▲ Some Mogul riches occasionally reached the ordinary people. Here Emperor Jahangir weighs Prince Khurram, in order that the equivalent of the Prince's weight in gold and silver might be distributed among his subjects.

The story of the building of the Taj Mahal begins on a festival day in Agra in the year 1607. It was the New Year's Fair at the Royal Meena Bazaar, a private marketplace in the palace gardens. In many Muslim societies then, as today, women spent most of their time indoors, only venturing outside if accompanied by a male relative and with their faces covered by a veil. For the women of the royal household, their only chance to meet and talk to men other than relatives was on "melas" or festival days at the Meena Bazaar. There the women sold trinkets at very high prices to nobles and courtiers. The story goes that the sixteen-year-old Prince Khurram stopped to haggle for gems at the stall of Arjumand Bano, the beautiful fifteen-year-old daughter of the prime minister, Asaf Khan. It was love at first sight.

Muslim law allowed every man up to four wives and many concubines. Princes were expected to marry into powerful families whose friendship was needed for political reasons. Therefore, Prince Khurram had to marry a Persian princess before he could marry Arjumand Bano. Five years later, never having laid eyes on her since that day at the bazaar in 1607, he was allowed to marry the girl with whom he had fallen in love.

▼ Shah Jahan and his favorite wife, Mumtaz Mahal. Entranced by her aristocratic beauty and quick wit, Shah Jahan lavished gifts upon Mumtaz; he also relied on her for political guidance, entrusting her with the state seal.

Emperor Jahangir was so pleased with his son's choice of wife that he placed the betrothal ring on her finger himself. On their wedding day in 1612, a great procession was followed by a ceremony that took place at the home of the bride, as is the Muslim custom. At midnight a gigantic feast was given, honored by the presence of Emperor Jahangir himself. There Jahangir gave Arjumand Bano the title Mumtaz Mahal, meaning "Exalted One of the Palace."

Wedding tradition
It is a Muslim and Hindu tradition for brides and grooms to have their hands decorated with beautiful patterns on their wedding day. The patterns are painted with a paste called *mehendi*, made of henna powder and turmeric.

Although the start to his marriage was blissful, Khurram's life as a prince was less than harmonious. Plotters at court threatened to destroy him. Jahangir's favorite wife, Nur Mahal, had been scheming to place one of her own children, Khurram's half-brother, on the throne after her husband's death. Realizing that his life was in danger, Khurram fled the court and gathered his own army.

By the time his father died in 1627, Khurram had the support of powerful men in the imperial army. Nur Mahal and her son were defeated and, in 1628, the exiled prince and Mumtaz Mahal declared themselves rulers of India. On his coronation, Prince Khurram took a new name to reflect his high status—Shah Jahan, or "King of the World."

The Mogul court was based in three cities: Agra, Delhi, and Lahore. But the new emperor ruled over a vast dominion that stretched from Assam in the east to Qandahar in the west; from the Upper Deccan in the south to the Pamir Mountains in the north. He gave generous gifts to his loyal followers—jade drinking cups, elephants, and daggers encrusted with gems. Enemies and potential rivals for the throne (including his remaining brothers and other male relatives) were executed.

▼ This map shows the dominion that Shah Jahan came to inherit at his accession.

Although Shah Jahan had other wives and concubines, Mumtaz Mahal was the great love of his life. Only she bore him children, and she went with him on all his travels, even when pregnant. She became his most trusted adviser and persuaded him to share her deep concern for people in need. Every morning, she distributed money and food to the poor who, starving and desperate, flocked to the palace gates. She drew up lists of widows, orphans, and the disabled so that the emperor could ensure that they were provided for.

◀ This beautifully inscribed drinking cup is made of jade and was used at the Mogul court.

◀ Shah Jahan loved beautiful things, especially jewels. Paintings from the time show him wearing jeweled turban ornaments, ropes of pearls, armlets, thumb rings, and belts studded with gems. His sword had a jeweled hilt and rested in a scabbard set with precious stones. In this illustration, Shah Jahan accepts a gift of pearls from Asaf Khan, his prime minister.

The royal poets wrote of Mumtaz Mahal's grace and beauty: her loveliness made the moon hide its face in shame. During nineteen years of marriage, Mumtaz Mahal gave birth to fourteen children, only seven of whom survived.

In 1631, Shah Jahan was engaged in a military campaign outside the city of Bhurhanpur. In the harem of the temporary encampment, Mumtaz Mahal lay dying, having just given birth to a healthy baby girl. Along with Wazir Khan and Sati-un-nissa, Shah Jahan sat by his wife's bedside and watched helplessly as her life ebbed away.

With Mumtaz Mahal at his side Shah Jahan had strengthened the empire, adding to it parts of the Deccan, and gaining from them wealth for the imperial treasury. After her death, however, he seemed to lose interest in warfare. It is reported that he locked himself in his rooms for eight days, refusing all food. Legend says that when he emerged his back was bent like an old man's, and his hair and beard had turned completely white.

▼ After the death of Mumtaz Mahal, Shah Jahan spent much of his time supervising the building of his new capital city Shahjahanabad (now Old Delhi). The Red Fort he built still stands in the center of Old Delhi, a magnificent reminder of the imperial past.

▲ The Pearl Mosque in Agra is built entirely out of white marble, except for a floor inlaid with yellow marble and an inscription in black above the entrance.

Perhaps to overcome his grief, Shah Jahan now focused his mind upon great building projects. His reign is believed to mark the height of Mogul architectural genius. At Delhi, he supervised the construction of the Red Fort and the Jami Masjid, one of the largest mosques ever built in India.

At the Red Fort at Agra he built the Pearl Mosque. He also carried out many changes to the fort itself, replacing much of the original sandstone with white marble inlaid with precious stones. Like his forefathers, he devoted his time to building pleasure pavilions, gardens, and mausoleums, including a project that would dominate the rest of his life, an exquisite shrine to his dead wife—the Taj Mahal.

CHAPTER THREE

THE PLAN FOR THE TAJ MAHAL

Shah Jahan decided that the Taj Mahal would be built on a site occupied by sprawling gardens on a bend in the left bank of the Yamuna River. The gardens were owned by a Hindu raja, to whom he gave four regal residences in exchange. Shah Jahan might have chosen the site for its beauty and because there was a clear view of it from the imperial palace at the Red Fort. It was close to Agra; perhaps he wanted the monument he was planning to be part of the community—a quiet, sacred place amid the noise and bustle of the city.

◀ The Taj Mahal was planned with such skill and care that even when the river floods, the plinth on which the mausoleum rests is always clear of the water. Even in the exceptional floods of 1924 and 1978 it remained untouched. If the plinth had been built any higher, though, the view of the Taj Mahal from boats on the river would have been distorted.

Legend has it that on her deathbed Mumtaz Mahal had asked Shah Jahan to build over her "such a temple as the world never saw." Very soon after her death, word reached the borders of India and lands beyond that the grief-stricken emperor was searching for an architect to build a magnificent tomb in memory of his beloved wife.

The Taj Mahal complex
This drawing, based on a nineteenth-century plan, shows the symmetrical design of the Taj Mahal and its grounds, and the other buildings in the complex. The design of the garden is based on the Persian *chahar bagh* (four-part garden), which is cut into quarters by water channels. Each quarter of the Taj Mahal garden is again divided, by paths, into four smaller sections.

1. Exterior gateway
2. Courtyard
3. Main gateway
4. Gardens
5. Mausoleum
6. Mosque
7. Rest house

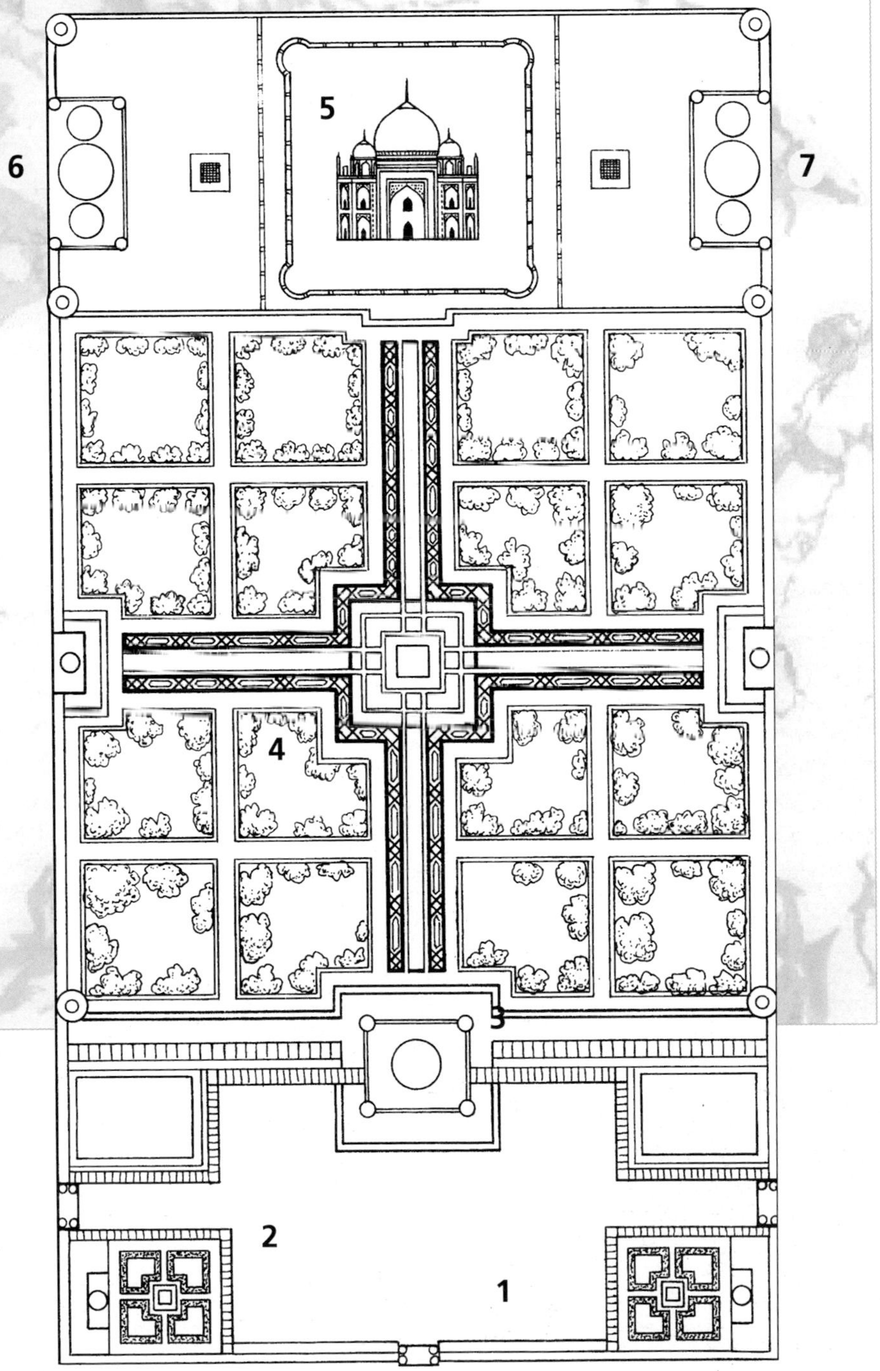

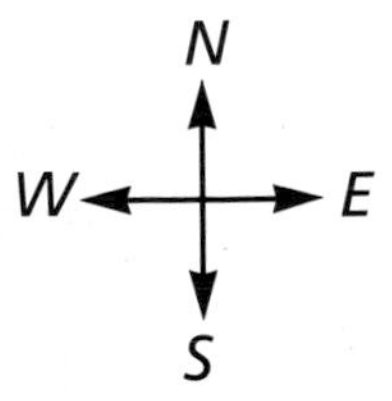

The Taj Mahal was designed by several architects under the direction of Shah Jahan himself and his chief architect, Ustad Ahmad, a Persian engineer. After drawing up detailed plans, the architects discussed them with master craftsmen, such as stonemasons and calligraphers.

The art of calligraphy was an important characteristic of Muslim architecture. The calligrapher Amanat Khan Shirazi had the job of decorating the walls of the Taj Mahal with Arabic lettering. It was unusual for craftsmen to sign their work, but Hanif of Baghdad, the master mason, and Amanat Khan were given permission to do so. Two extra calligraphers, famous for their fine work, were brought to Agra to assist the master calligrapher, together with the most skillful stonecutters. In all, there were 37 stonecutters, each having his own special skill, such as carving flowers or cutting gems.

▼ This photograph shows workers cleaning the calligraphy on the exterior of the Taj Mahal. Below the black lettering can be seen beautiful floral patterns made of precious stones set into the marble, using a technique called *pietra dura*.

▲ The great dome of the Taj Mahal. In the nineteenth century, the British replaced the gold ornament with a brass finial.

The art of inlay work was perfected under the Moguls. At the Taj Mahal, floral patterns made of precious gems were cut into the marble. Mogul inlayers were so skilled that legend claims they could see through stone and cut gems with their eyes! Chiranji Lal from Delhi was chosen as the chief inlayer on the Taj Mahal.

Muslims believe the dome to be the most perfect shape on Earth. Shah Jahan wanted the best designer and builder to make the dome of the Taj Mahal. He chose Ismail Afandi from Turkey. On top of the dome would be a beautiful gold finial, cast by Qazim Khan, the famous metalworker from Lahore.

To make sure that every detail of every stage of the building was perfect, two high-ranking nobles were appointed to supervise the whole operation.

CHAPTER FOUR

BUILDING THE TAJ MAHAL

▼ As shown in this painting by Abanindranath Tagore, Shah Jahan was often present to oversee the work on the Taj Mahal.

By the time Mumtaz Mahal's body was brought back to Agra in 1631, Shah Jahan had approved the final plans for the Taj Mahal. A wooden model was made to show how the finished building would look. Before building work began, the Yamuna River was diverted so that the view from the finished tomb would be improved. Then workers cleared an area the size of three football fields, which they dug out for the foundations and filled with sediment. This ensured that no water from the river could seep into the building.

Thousands of laborers, craftspeople, and artists began to flock to Agra. In the 22 years it took to complete the Taj Mahal, 20,000 people were employed. Houses were needed for the workers who came, not only from India, but also from distant parts of the Mogul empire, places such as Baghdad, Samarkand, Constantinople, and Kandahar. A new suburb of Agra grew up around the unfinished Taj Mahal. It was called Mumtazabad in honor of the dead queen.

Shah Jahan had decided that the mausoleum would be built of white marble. He chose the unusual blue-veined marble from quarries at Makrana, near Jodhpur. Red sandstone from Akbar's now abandoned city of Fatehpur Sikri was used for the garden walls, entry arch, mosque, and rest house. Just as the best craftspeople were brought to Agra, so were the best materials: jade and crystal from China, turquoise from Tibet, and lapis lazuli from Afghanistan. Forty-three different types of gems were ultimately used to decorate the Taj Mahal.

▼ The blue-veined marble can clearly be seen on the lower terrace surrounding the Taj Mahal. Here it is laid with red sandstone in a geometric design.

▼ The Taj Mahal seen from the south, over the suburbs of Agra. The large, red sandstone building visible to the left of the Taj is the main gateway.

A road ramp made of trampled earth was built, stretching right through the city of Agra and up to the site of the Taj Mahal. Along this 10-mi. (16-km) ramp traveled carts carrying heavy slabs of marble and sandstone.

In the 1640s Father Manrique, a Portuguese friar, described the building work as "still incomplete, the greater part of it remaining to be done." Along the route to Agra he saw great blocks of marble:

"... of such unusual size and length that they drew the sweat of many powerful teams of oxen and of fierce-looking, big-horned buffaloes, which were dragging enormous, strongly made wagons, in teams of twenty or thirty animals...."

At the site, the blocks of stone had to be lifted to build the walls. This meant raising them eventually to a height of almost 250 ft. (76 m). To do this, a post-and-beam pulley was built, worked by teams of men and mules who pulled the ropes.

◀ Like the laborers who worked on the Taj Mahal, these women builders in Agra today are passing materials from hand to hand. Paintings from the time record that women worked alongside men on the building.

Building the Taj Mahal
1. Post-and-beam pulley
2. Marble blocks
3. Ramp
4. Decorating the walls
5. Scaffolding

▼ The Taj Mahal's adjacent buildings and gardens are constructed with exquisite symmetry.

CHAPTER FIVE

THE TAJ MAHAL COMPLETED

The first buildings in the Taj Mahal complex to be completed were the tomb itself and the two side buildings. Next came the four minarets, and finally the gateway and remaining buildings. Everything was constructed to harmonize completely, because Islamic law states that once a building has been raised nothing more can ever be added to it or taken away from it.

◀ Once the mausoleum of the Taj Mahal was completed in around 1652, Shah Jahan spent most of his time in Delhi, supervising work on other buildings. This nineteenth-century engraving shows him leaving the Great Mosque at Delhi by elephant.

Every year Shah Jahan commemorated the anniversary of Mumtaz Mahal's death with feasting and gifts. As time went on, he gave his four eldest sons responsibility for military matters in different parts of the empire, relying increasingly on his favorite, the eldest, Dara Shikoh. In 1655 he appeared to honor Dara as his chosen successor by presenting him with a jewel-studded robe of honor and asking him to sit in a golden chair beside his own Peacock Throne.

In 1657 Shah Jahan fell ill, and his other three sons, Aurangzeb, Murad, and Shuja, began plotting to seize the throne. When Shah Jahan decided to return to Agra to die in sight of the Taj Mahal, Dara went with him. They left Delhi on October 18 and on November 5 arrived about six mi. (10 km) up the Yamuna River from Agra, where they set up camp. Court astrologers had advised that the best day to enter Agra was November 26. On that day, amid the prayers and blessings of crowds of people lining the river banks, the royal barge carried Shah Jahan down the river to the Red Fort.

"My child, I have decided not to do any important business or decide on any great undertaking ... without your knowledge and without consulting you first.... I cannot sufficiently thank Allah for blessing me with a son like you."

Shah Jahan's words to Dara Shikoh

The peace that Shah Jahan had hoped for in Agra was not to be found, for now the rivalry between his sons broke out into open hostility. Aurangzeb struck first, throwing Murad into prison where, three years later, he was put to death. Shuja was killed, but the details of his death remain a mystery. Dara was imprisoned and eventually executed. Finally, Aurangzeb turned on his father. In 1658 he entered Agra with his army, imprisoned Shah Jahan in the Red Fort, and crowned himself emperor.

For eight years, Shah Jahan remained in his rooms at the Red Fort, a prisoner of his own son. By January 1666, he was very ill. He lay on a simple bed in the Jasmine

▼ The imprisoned Shah Jahan would have gazed upon the Taj Mahal from this vantage point at the Red Fort in Agra.

Tower, looking out across the river at the Taj Mahal turning pale rose in the setting sun. The dying emperor murmured a Muslim confession of faith: "O God! make my condition good in this world and the next, and save me from the torments of hellfire." His daughter Jahanara read some verses from the Koran to him. The emperor died gazing at his most beautiful creation, the distant image of his wife's tomb.

▲ Aurangzeb, shown here at prayer, was a devout Muslim and an energetic and brave soldier; but by the end of his reign of 49 years the Mogul empire had begun to crumble.

Shah Jahan had told Jahanara that he wanted to be buried beside Mumtaz Mahal. His body was prepared for an immediate funeral and placed in a sandalwood coffin. Jahanara had hoped for a great procession to take her father to his final resting place, but Aurangzeb sent no such instruction. The weeping Jahanara and a few court officials were the only mourners in the small group of boats taking the coffin along the river to the Taj Mahal. But once the people of Agra heard of Shah Jahan's death, they grieved for the emperor they had loved. Court records tell us that "the cry of lamentation rose up from every house, in the lanes and market-places alike." The final irony of Shah Jahan's life was that he never lived to see the Taj Mahal complex completed; work there finished in 1667, one year after his death.

CHAPTER SIX

A VISIT TO THE TAJ MAHAL

A visit to the Taj Mahal is still a thrilling experience, despite the passage of time and the recent effects of pollution from nearby factories upon the marble exterior. In the seventeenth century, Shah Jahan and members of the imperial family would have approached the Taj Mahal from the river. Then, as today, other visitors would have approached it from the south through the courtyard. From this direction Shah Jahan's workers approached their near-completed masterpiece each day.

▼ The main gateway to the Taj Mahal is a three-story building crowned with eleven "kiosks." Its function was to safeguard the gold and gems that decorated the monument within.

In the courtyard the huge, red sandstone gateway rises to a height of over 100 ft. (30 m). This gateway was among the last buildings of the Taj Mahal complex to be completed. It is etched in black calligraphy with selected verses from the Koran. Originally, the gateway was lined with silver plating to complement the whiteness of the Taj Mahal, but the silver was stolen in the eighteenth century. It has since been replaced with copper, a cheaper metal.

Through the gateway, the visitors of ancient times would have seen a garden full of flowers, with paths leading through beds of colorful and sweet-smelling blooms. Today, however, the visitor sees lush, green lawns and paths alongside pools leading toward the white marble mausoleum. Here, as in traditional Mogul gardens, water is an important part of the design. A long rectangular pool of water adds another dimension to the symmetry by providing a perfect reflection of the central building.

▼ Here the long pool is used to water the lawns and gardens. Today, because of a shortage of water in this part of India, the fountains play only for an hour every evening.

The Taj Mahal itself stands in the middle of a massive marble platform almost 315 ft. (96 m) square. At each corner of the platform is a minaret—a slender, tapered tower rising to 138 ft. (42 m) in height. The minarets have been described as "an accepted prayer ascending to heaven from a pious heart," and were used to call the faithful to prayer. They were built slanting outward slightly, so that if they collapsed they would not damage the Taj Mahal.

"These four thin tapering towers standing at the four corners of the platform on which the Taj is built are among the ugliest structures ever erected by human hands."

Aldous Huxley, English novelist and one of the few visitors to find little of beauty in the Taj Mahal

▶ The famous minarets are crowned with eight windowed cupolas. People are no longer allowed inside them, and their only inhabitants today are colonies of bats.

▲ The domes, arches, and minarets of the Taj Mahal are repeated in the two side buildings. These identical red sandstone structures are important to the symmetry of the Taj Mahal complex as a whole.

The Taj itself is square, with the corners cut away, or chamfered. On each of the mausoleum's identical facades, or sides, is an arch 110 ft. (33 m) high. Flower designs are sculpted on the marble walls of the main archways. From a distance, the Taj Mahal appears completely white, but a closer look reveals intricate decoration, including black marble calligraphy from the Koran and colorful floral inlay work. The world-famous central dome is onion-shaped and stands 200 ft. (61 m) high. It is held aloft by four eight-sided, domed towers, which stand at each of the Taj Mahal's corners. The inside faces of these towers are linked together so that they support the huge weight of the central dome.

▶ An exquisitely carved marble panel on the facade of the Taj Mahal

Following the Indian custom of showing respect to holy places, visitors remove their shoes as they enter the Taj Mahal itself. In the center of the building, under the main dome, lies the burial chamber of Mumtaz Mahal and Shah Jahan. This huge, eight-sided room is surrounded by eight empty chambers, four rectangular and four eight-sided, which help support the heavy marble dome. The eight-sided chambers were originally intended for the remains of Shah Jahan's relatives, but they have remained empty to this day.

▼ This vertical section through the Taj Mahal shows a central chamber surrounded by two stories of eight rooms with connecting passageways. This is a traditional Mogul design called *hasht behist,* or "eight paradises." The dome makes a third story. The real tombs are underground. The tops of the minarets are exactly level with the widest part of the dome, to emphasize its great size.

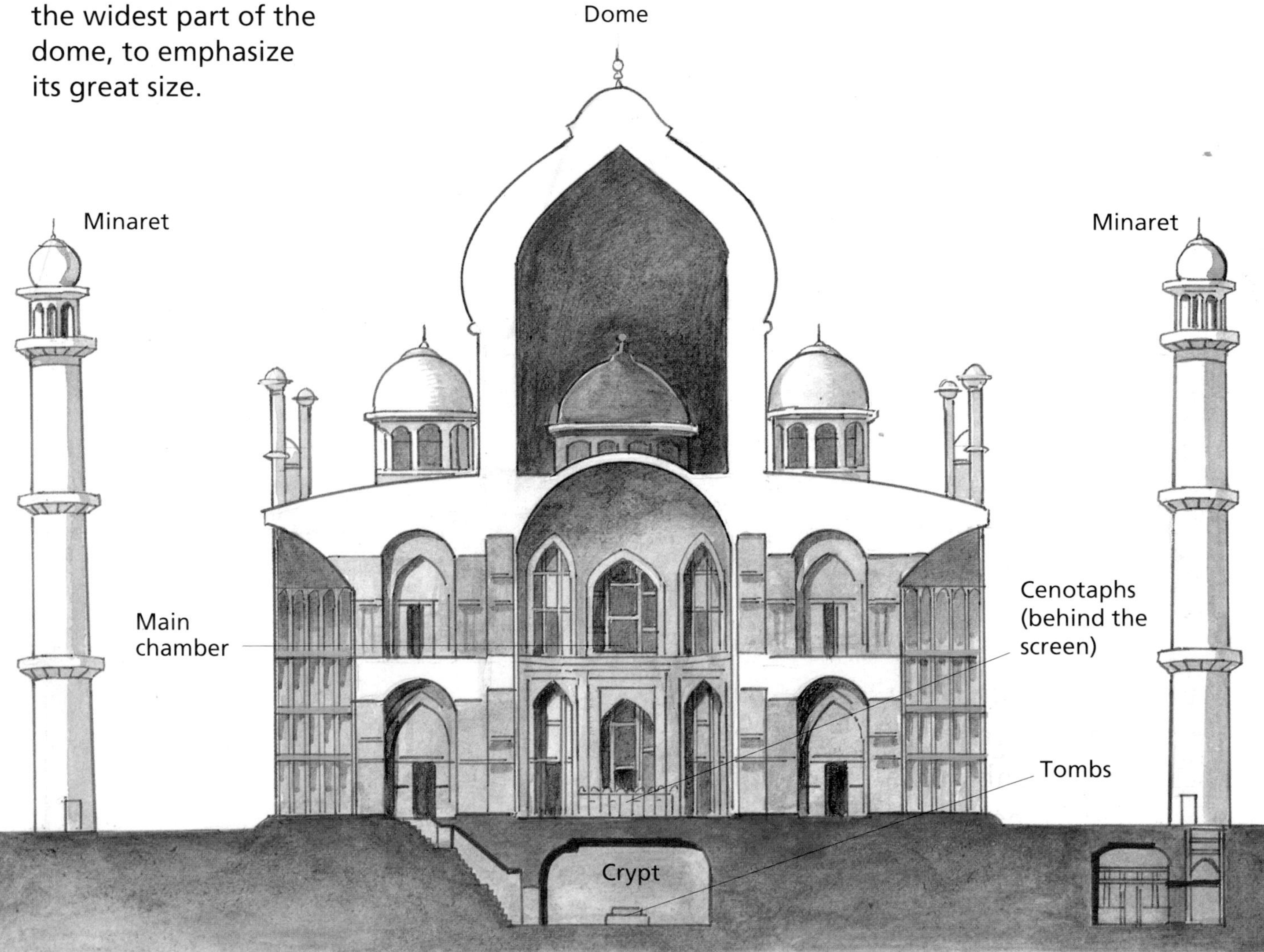

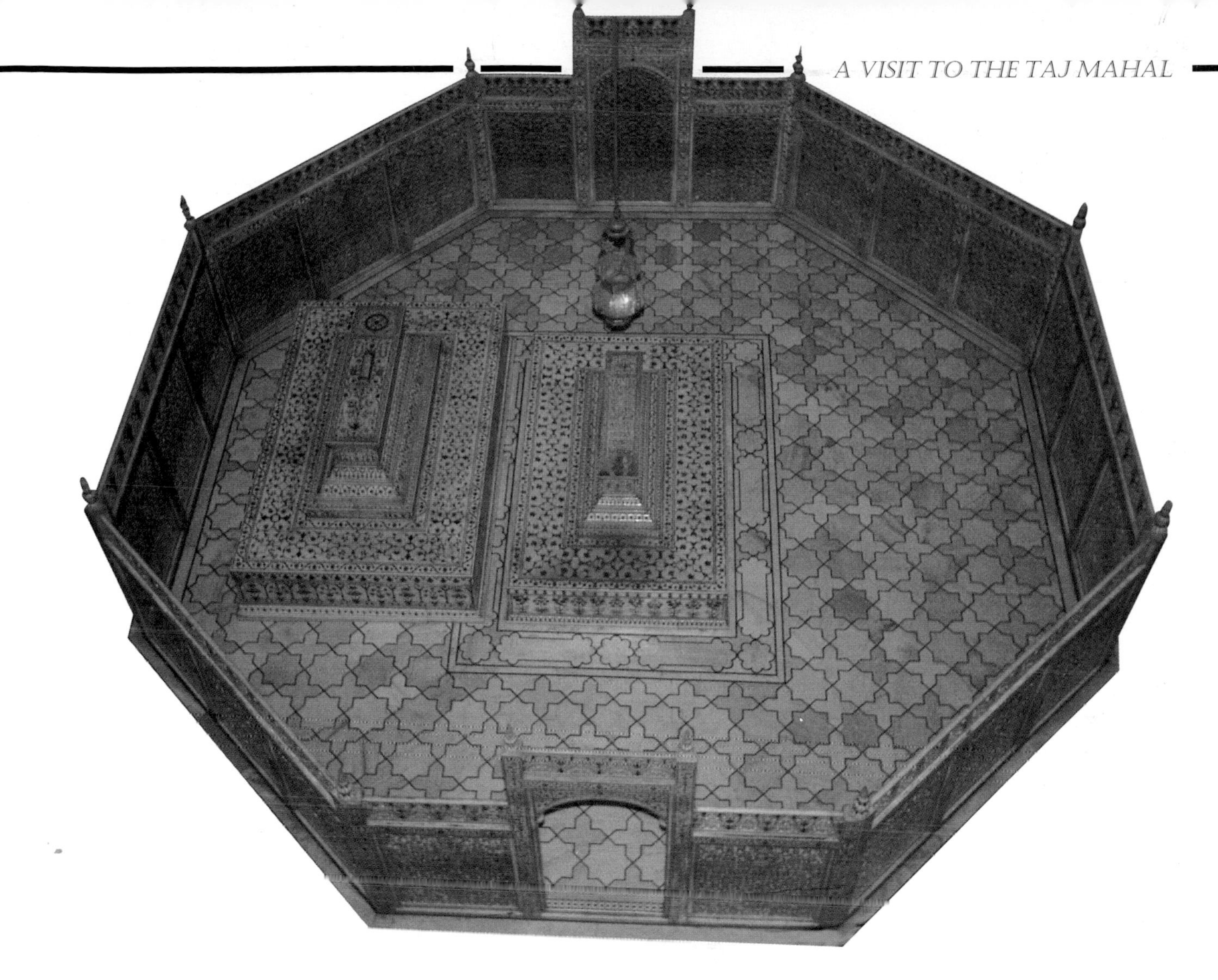

▲ The octagonal main chamber with Mumtaz Mahal's tomb perfectly centered, and Shah Jahan's squeezed in beside it.

In the center of the main chamber is the tomb of Mumtaz Mahal and to one side of it is the tomb of the emperor. These tombs (or cenotaphs) are false, as the bodies of the emperor and his queen are buried in a small crypt directly beneath the main chamber. On Mumtaz Mahal's cenotaph are verses from the Koran in Islamic calligraphy, cut from black marble and meticulously inlaid.

Shah Jahan's burial in the Taj Mahal disturbed the perfect symmetry of the building. There is a story that, for his own tomb, Shah Jahan had planned to build a copy of the Taj Mahal in black marble on the opposite bank of the river, but no plans or excavations for it have been found. Instead, under the order of his son Aurangzeb, his tomb was squeezed in next to Mumtaz Mahal's.

Features such as domes, arches, niches, and decorations are repeated in different sizes and situations throughout the building. The lower sections (dados) of each of the eight walls in the main chamber have panels decorated with sculpted flowers and surrounded by borders with *pietra dura* flower designs. Over each panel is an arch with more inlaid flower patterns above it and calligraphy from the Koran surrounding it. These features echo the decoration on the exterior of the building.

The cenotaphs were originally enclosed by a gold railing, studded with jewels and valued at six hundred thousand rupees. It was removed in 1642, possibly because it might attract vandals, but more probably because Shah Jahan saw that it was too ornate for its surroundings.

▼ The railing around the cenotaphs was replaced in 1642 with an octagonal lattice screen. The marble of the screen is carved so finely that it resembles lace.

Floral inlays
The cenotaphs are of white marble, decorated with floral designs cut from gemstones: rubies, emeralds, turquoise, lapis lazuli, jasper, carnelian, jade, amethyst, agate, chalcedony, quartz, and sardonyx. These stones are set into the marble, using the technique known as *pietra dura*, which is employed throughout the Taj Mahal.

The screen that replaced the railing surrounding the two cenotaphs apparently took ten years to carve. It is decorated with *pietra dura* floral designs more elaborate than any other in the building. The flowers, vines, and fruit depicted upon it are Islamic symbols of the rewards for those who enter paradise. The chamber is lit softly and naturally by a latticework of marble screens. This filtered light helps to create the spiritual atmosphere of the building, giving the highest parts of the dome a misty appearance.

"The wonder of wonders is the white grille that stands in the center of the translucent hall.... It is made of plaques of marble placed upright, so finely worked that it might be thought that they were carved in ivory."

Pierre Loti, French novelist, 1903

At one time musicians came to play music in the antechambers of the Taj Mahal. The acoustics there and in the main chamber are wonderfully resonant. Today, only the quiet rustling of clothing and the murmur of prayers and verses from the Koran are heard. The design of the building makes the murmured prayers reverberate around the chamber and the passages. The sound of voices may echo for many minutes, gradually rising to silence in the heights of the dome.

CHAPTER SEVEN

A PLACE OF PILGRIMAGE AND ROMANCE

"Prayers here are answered, it is in fact the very spot where worship meets with a favorable reception.... Should a sinner enter this mansion, he will be cleansed from his sins."

These words, written by Shah Jahan, suggest how he envisaged the Taj Mahal would be used. As well as serving its purpose as a *rauza* (tomb), he also intended that the building be an *urs* (a place of pilgrimage). However, after his death Mogul fortunes began to wane. Aurangzeb pursued endless costly wars; his empire had become too big and was very difficult to govern. There were eleven more Mogul rulers after Aurangzeb, all of them presiding over an empire in decline.

◀ A drawing from 1825 shows crowds strolling in the grounds of the Royal Pavilion at Brighton, England. The influence of the Taj Mahal is evident in the pavilion's domes and minarets.

▶ This impressionistic view of the Taj Mahal, painted in the nineteenth century by Hercules Brabazon, shows an overgrown garden with huge trees obscuring the building.

By the eighteenth century, the Taj Mahal was suffering from neglect. A target for vandals, it was plundered for gold, silver, and jewels, and the gardens gradually became overgrown. After Robert Clive's victory on the fields of Plassey near Calcutta in 1757, British travelers began to visit India. The buildings they saw there influenced architecture in Great Britain. Cockerell's design for Sezincote in Gloucestershire was based on the Taj Mahal, as was the Brighton Pavilion, designed by Repton and Nash.

During the nineteenth century, the British took complete control of India. English visitors held moonlit picnics at the Taj Mahal, and lovers used it as a meeting place. Brass bands played on the marble terrace outside the main door, and the mosque and rest house on either side of the mausoleum were rented to honeymooners.

"At an earlier date, when picnic parties were held in the garden of the Taj, it was not an uncommon thing for the revelers to arm themselves with hammer and chisel, with which they whiled away the afternoon by chipping out fragments of agate and carnelian from the cenotaphs of the Emperor and his lamented Queen."

Lord Curzon, viceroy of India in the early twentieth century

> "The Taj Mahal is not a building. It is a prayer, breathing in the night like the moon. At dusk it glows, whole swollen gold against the nighting sky."
>
> William Congdon, American artist, 1955

By the beginning of the twentieth century there was a growing appreciation of Indian art, and Lord Curzon had begun to restore what remained of the Mogul buildings. At the Taj Mahal, local craftspeople were hired to cut marble and repair the damaged *pietra dura*. In the grounds, the stone channels were dug out, and flowerbeds and avenues of trees were replanted.

The Taj Mahal was once again appreciated as a work of architectural genius. Poets, writers, and artists were inspired by it; even wallpaper and crockery showed its influence.

Small models of the Taj Mahal were shipped to Europe and America as souvenirs. A large wooden model of the Taj Mahal was carved for a jeweler in Agra. It found its way to an exhibition in Paris, after which it was taken, in 1939, to New York for the World's Fair. As if to confirm its eternal appeal, countless restaurants in Europe and America have adopted the name "Taj Mahal" over the years.

The Taj Mahal still attracts many thousands of visitors each year. What has given it such lasting popularity? One reason is that it is a symbol of excellence. All the materials used were carefully chosen, and every part of the design was based on meticulous research and planning. Another reason is its air of spirituality, the link between an earthly and a heavenly paradise. A third reason—and for many the most compelling—is its intensely romantic quality. It was inspired by grief and love and built to preserve the memory of one woman. No woman before or since has inspired such a memorial.

▼ The Taj Mahal, seen at sunset across the Yamuna River

TIME LINE

1450–1530

1484 Birth of Babur in Farghana, Turkey

1508 Birth of Humayun

1519 Babur invades India and seizes Bajaur

1525 Babur sets out to conquer Delhi. In 1526 he succeeds and also takes most of the Punjab. He founds the Mogul dynasty

1530–1550

1530 Death of Babur; Humayun becomes Mogul emperor

1533-39 Humayun's empire attacked by Afghans, led by Sher Khan

1539 Afghan ruler, Sher Khan (Sher Shah) captures Mogul empire from Humayun

1542 Birth of Akbar

1550–1600

1555 Humayun recaptures the Mogul empire in India and is back on the throne in Delhi

1556 Death of Humayun; Akbar succeeds him

1565 Construction of Red Fort at Agra begins

1569 Birth of Salim (Jahangir)

1570 Construction of Fatehpur Sikri begins

1592 Birth of Prince Khurram (Shah Jahan)

1593 Birth of Arjumand Bano (Mumtaz Mahal)

1600–1650

1605 Death of Akbar; Jahangir succeeds him

1612 Marriage of Prince Khurram (Shah Jahan) and Mumtaz Mahal

1614 Birth of Jahanara

1615 Birth of Dara Shikoh

1616 Birth of Shuja

1618 Birth of Aurangzeb

1624 Birth of Murad

1627 Death of Jahangir

1628 Shah Jahan becomes Mogul emperor

1631 Death of Mumtaz Mahal

1632 Building of the Taj Mahal begins

1650–1700

1652 Shah Jahan moves to Delhi

1657 Shah Jahan returns to Agra

1658 Aurangzeb seizes the Red Fort and imprisons Shah Jahan

1659 Death of Dara Shikoh

1661 Deaths of Shuja and Murad

1666 Death of Shah Jahan

1667 Taj Mahal completed

1700–1800

1707 Death of Aurangzeb

1757 British, led by Robert Clive, win Battle of Plassey (Bengal)

1800–1850

1820 Most of India under British rule

1849 British take control of the Punjab

1850–PRESENT DAY

1899–1905 Lord Curzon begins restoration at Taj Mahal

1939 Model of Taj Mahal used in the India exhibition at the World's Fair in New York

1947 India wins independence

GLOSSARY

Chronicle
An account of events written in the order in which they took place.

Concubine
A woman treated as a wife by a man who is not her husband. In Mogul society there were several concubines in the same household as well as one or more wives.

Crypt
An underground chamber in which bodies are buried.

Cupola
A small, domelike structure on top of a roof or tower.

Finial
An ornament, sometimes urn-shaped, used to decorate a roof or wall.

Harem
The part of a Muslim household in which women live.

Howdah
A seat with a canopy for riding on an elephant's back.

Kiosk
A small structure open at the sides.

Mausoleum
A large tomb.

Minaret
A tower, usually part of a mosque, from which the call to prayer is sounded.

Mosque
A building in which Muslims worship.

Niche
A hollow in a wall, often in the shape of an arch.

Octagonal
Eight-sided.

Pavilion
A building in which people are entertained.

Plinth
A base, or low platform.

Poll tax
A tax paid by each person.

Raja
A king or prince in India.

Retinue
A group of attendants or followers.

Symmetry
A similarity of form. If an imaginary line were to be drawn through the Taj Mahal, the parts on each side of the line would correspond exactly. The building is therefore said to have perfect symmetry.

FURTHER INFORMATION

BOOKS

Cumming, David. *The Ganges Delta and Its People* (People & Places). Austin, TX: Raintree Steck-Vaughn, 1994.

Ganeri, Anita. *Exploration into India.* Parsippany, NJ: Silver Burdett Press, 1994.

—— & Jonardon Ganeri. *India* (Country Fact Files). Austin, TX: Raintree Steck-Vaughn, 1995.

Haskins, James. *India Under Indira and Rajiv Gandhi.* Springfield, NJ: Enslow Publishers, 1989.

Lerner Publications. Department of Geography Staff. *India in Pictures.* Minneapolis, MN: Lerner Group, 1995.

McNair, Sylvia. *India* (Enchantment of the World). Danbury, CT: Children's Press, 1990.

Srinivasan, Rodbika. *India* (Cultures of the World). Tarrytown, NY: Marshall Cavendish, 1991.

Picture acknowledgments
The publishers would like to thank the following for allowing their pictures to be reproduced: Ancient Art & Architecture Collection: page 29; Bridgeman Art Library: pages 6 (Victoria and Albert Museum), 13 (British Library), 28, 31 (Bibliothèque Nationale), 35 (top), 41; Mary Evans Picture Library: pages 24, 40; Werner Forman Archive: page 8; Christina Gascoigne Photographs: pages 10 (left), 12, 16, 25 (top), 26; Global Scenes: pages 44, 45; Angelo Hornak Photograph Library: pages 7 (V & A), 10 (right, V & A), 11 (V & A); Ann & Bury Peerless Picture Library: pages 3, 5, 14, 17, 19, 20, 23, 30, 34, 35 (bottom), 37, 38, 39; Tony Stone Images: front cover (David Sutherland), pages 9 (Gavin Hellier), 18–19 (Alan Smith), 22 (Hugh Sitton), 25 (bottom, Gavin Hellier), 32 (Alan Smith), 33 (Suzanne & Nick Geary), 42–43 (Glen Allison); Wayland Picture Library: page 15.

INDEX

Numbers in **bold** refer to illustrations.

© Copyright 1997 Wayland (Publishers) Ltd.

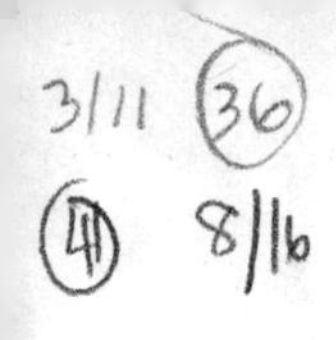